miscellaneous female

Recordings by the author

Shadows Wake Me
Hyperdramatic
Davnet

with Shaye
The Bridge

miscellaneous female

the journals of
Damhnait Doyle

INSOMNIAC PRESS

Copyright © 2005 by Damhnait Doyle

All rights reserved. No part of this publication may be reproduced, stored in a retrieval system or transmitted, in any form or by any means, without the prior written permission of the publisher or, in case of photocopying or other reprographic copying, a license from Access Copyright, 1 Yonge Street, Suite 1900, Toronto, Ontario, Canada, M5E 1E5.

Library and Archives Canada Cataloguing in Publication

Doyle, Damhnait
  Miscellaneous female : the journals of Dahmnait Doyle.

ISBN 1-897178-01-8

  1. Doyle, Damhnait--Diaries. 2. Singers--Canada--Diaries.
I. Title. II. Title: Journals of Dahmnait Doyle.

ML420.D754A3 2005   782.42164'092   C2005-903403-3

The publisher gratefully acknowledges the support of the Canada Council, the Ontario Arts Council and the Department of Canadian Heritage through the Book Publishing Industry Development Program.

Printed and bound in Canada

Insomniac Press
192 Spadina Avenue, Suite 403
Toronto, Ontario, Canada, M5T 2C2
www.insomniacpress.com

Dedication

For my father, who taught me to laugh even if no one else is laughing.

For my mother, who taught me to always take the high road.

Introduction

It's 5:30 in the morning; the birds are singing, the sun is coming up, and I have just finished proofreading my life in print. It was quite intimidating to see three years of my innermost thoughts in one neat little bundle, sitting there staring at me. In a sense, that's where its title comes from. For, as women, regardless of our occupations and circumstances, we often follow similar paths; the beginnings, middles, and endings are parallel. Regardless of whether or not you are Buffy Sainte-Marie, Loreena McKennitt, or Sylvia Tyson, you are — as we were all identified on the dressing-room door at the Canadian Songwriters Hall of Fame Awards — a Miscellaneous Female.

February 18, 2003

I am back in Toronto after the East Coast Music Awards and I am excited and tired... Halifax was as per usual a complete blast and a bit of a blur. Saw some amazing bands like Mark Bragg, Wintersleep, and Buck 65. Crazy stuff going on music-wise at home and it's totally inspiring. It was a trip to play the awards show and to do it sitting on a bed — I have never been so relaxed while doing live TV. It was great to have my band out there with me, to have Kevin Fox, my partner in crime, singing away, and Joel Plaskett on banjo (he gave me a copy of his CD and it's pretty incredible).

I had fun Saturday night singing with my girls Saltwater Trio at our first real gig. Kim Stockwood, Tara MacLean, and I are in the middle of recording a CD that will be released next fall. We have been cutting tracks with Bill Bell (producer of Danko Jones) and Jay Joyce (producer of Patty Griffin) and will continue to record around my touring schedule, Tara's solo recording, and the baby in Kim's belly. It has really invigorated my love of making and recording music. I can't even begin to explain how fun it is for us (and scary for others) when we get together and have a little caffeine in the studio!

I went today and saw the video for "Another California Song" today and it's so freakin' cool.

Benji Weinstein directed it and did a remarkable job. The girls sing on the track and have roles in the video — Kim as the motel receptionist and Tara as my captive! The idea is that Tara is my boyfriend's new girlfriend and I steal her, throw her in the trunk, take her to the motel, and tie her up. Again, the most fun I've had on any video and it looks fabulous...

I'm doing laundry, unpacking my new apartment, and getting ready to go on tour tomorrow afternoon. I'm off to Vancouver for the Bluebird North tour with Sarah Slean, Danny Michel, Choclair, Neil Osbourne, Blair Packham, and Shari Ulrich — it's going to be a blast and I can't wait to get back out on the road; it's been so long. I'll let you know how it goes!

March 4, 2003

Well, I am on the plane to Newfoundland and the tour is over. If anyone saw the Bluebird North show in these last two weeks, you will know what a fantastic time we had! What an eclectic group of people; if I had to make a list of whom I would invite to a dinner party, living or dead, I'd ask these people. We had so much fun playing, contributing to each other's songs, and, of course, dancing on the bus for Dance Party USA (not only is Sarah Slean an unbelievable artist, that woman can boogie her ass off). We played in Halifax at Hell's Kitchen last night and, as we suspected, we blew out the tour in fine form with much on- and off-stage tomfoolery, Jäger, and pizza.

It's funny, I haven't really toured in six years and this was a great way to ease myself back into it. Lesson #1: I need to bring a smaller suitcase — much, much smaller. It's really just the shoes I need to downsize since I usually end up wearing pretty much the same thing every show. You should see the amount of stuff I brought on this trip with me, very green indeed and a little like a travelling circus. Lesson #2: don't sleep all day on the bus or you won't be able to sleep at night. Lesson #3: no matter how hungry you are after the gig, *never* eat Thai green chicken curry at 1 a.m. or you will have horrible nightmares about things I can't mention here. Lesson #4: bring

Neil Osbourne with you to every gig so he will strongly encourage people to buy your brand-new CD because people listen to Neil!

I am home for a week of supposed rest but I am going out tonight to see Sarah Slean at the Ship Inn, where I played my first gig!

March 22, 2003

Good thoughts...love life
Breathe deeply
Feet firmly, solid on the ground
Hot bath...wash it all away
New book...new

I feel left out of the misery
Baking under the hot sun
The sun burns my eyes as
You all grow cold
It's no fun being young
When all your friends are acting old
Watch my face as it does nothing at all
Only my hands betray my evolve

April 21, 2003

Well, I am in Regina after a long bus ride from Calgary and I must say five shows in four days is tiring! I am about ten days into the Tom Cochrane tour and I am having a blast. Tom, Red Rider, and their crew are amazing — truly giving, and we are having such a great time on the road. The shows have been fantastic: some theatres, some arenas, and all crazy fans of Tom Cochrane and Red Rider (and, maybe, some new fans). I hope that some of you reading this are the *great* people who have bought my records at shows these last two weeks. Thank you so much.

There are a few things I have learned of late. First, never announce to an arena full of people that you like tequila because you may never be able to walk again without hurting people's feelings. Second, learn the words to your favourite songs before you attempt to sing them at the late-night bus jam. Third, when travelling on a bus with eleven men and you are the lone female, bring pictures of your favourite women such as your mother, grandmother, sister, girl bandmates to remind yourself that other life forms exist. Also, never build a Tiki hut without good wind coverage. And finally, never go anywhere without Kevin Fox — the man who will sing and play like an angel and keep the ladies in the front happy!

April 23, 2003

Well, the first leg of the Tom Cochrane and Red Rider tour is over; I am exhausted but mostly sad. Funny that not two weeks ago I was so shy and reserved that I asked Kevin to enter the tour bus before me so I could ease my way in. Well now we have finished in Regina — Red Rider and crew have headed to the States and we fly to T.O. tomorrow.

Not since I played the founder of the Sisters of Mercy for an international (habit-wearing) nun convention have I hugged so many people and felt so connected. What a *great* group of people who are now friends. I can't wait until May 1st in Hamilton to start it all over again (and work on my abs singing "No Regrets" and "Life Is a Highway"). In the meantime, I go into the studio tomorrow night with Kim and Tara to finish our trio record with the fantastic Jay Joyce.

I am looking forward to hanging with my sisters (my real live sis lives in England — hey, Ceara) and catching up — their friendship makes life so much easier... Wow, the video stations play great music late at night: the incomparable Kathleen Edwards, new Matthew Good, and now Big Wreck — gotta love it!

I'm looking forward to playing as a four piece in Ottawa Saturday night at Barrymore's for Atlantic Scene and then the ECMA Songwriter's Circle on

Sunday — Gordie Sampson is gonna be there; his new record is going to blow people's minds!

    I love my parents for raising me in a way that allows me to embrace the long awaited good times — oh, and lending me money to make my record (don't worry, I paid them back).

love dav
XOXOXOXOXOXOXOXOXOXOXOXOX-
OXOXOXOXOXOX

August 21, 2003

It's been so long since I have written and so much has happened — I don't know where to begin. It's funny that I have such an aversion to computers and the changing ways of the world while my brother, sister, and father are computer freaks (I guess I take after my mother in that regard). It's a little like going to the gym (diary entries that is) — hard as hell to get there, but when you do, you never want to stop...

I have been on the road all summer — why then, on the only days off I have in T.O. are there jackhammers *right* outside my window?! Now, I am not much of a morning person, I am up most nights until 3:00 or 4:00 reading, so I recoil at the prospect of jackhammers at 7:37 a.m. To keep me company while the sound of the jackhammer becomes a pulsing, rhythmic sound bite that carries me back to sleep I have made close friends with Neil Young, Steve Earle, and Johnny Cash in just a few weeks. Ah, the thrill of the rock and roll biography — stories so rich and implausible they'd be considered over the top for daytime TV.

The most thorough of the books is Neil Young's *Shakey* — the writing is stunning and effective. I went out and bought four of his records the day I finished and now feel a childlike connection to his music. My dad bought me the Steve Earle book; he became a fan after I toured

Canada with Steve in 1996. I remember the first show opening for Steve. Cory Tetford from Crush (who was playing guitar with me and singing back-up) and I were standing sidestage when he started to sing the song "Goodbye," which I recognized from Emmylou Harris' brilliant *Wrecking Ball* album. When I realized he had written that song, I settled in for two weeks' worth of disguised awe. As the book confirmed, I figured he wouldn't have dug someone walking around telling him how good he was when he had just a year previously cleaned up his act and gotten sober. Steve has gone on to do so much for raising awareness surrounding the archaic practice of capital punishment, his music is just a jumping-off point.

I finished Cash just half an hour ago and realized it's time for me to start writing again and maybe slack off a little on the reading, although I have another Carol Shields book that has my name written all over it. Coincidentally, I picked up my first Shields book, *Larry's Party*, the evening before she died and readily moved on to her latest novel, *Unless*, which refers to the lack of acknowledgement women writers receive when other writers (both men and women) cite their influences. My heart was warmed in Johnny Cash's book when he twice refers to his love of the poet Edna St. Vincent Millay and, of course, his love of his wife — a beautiful passage...

We played Massey Hall — Kevin Fox and myself opening for Tom Cochrane on May 10th. I wanted to write after that show, but found myself confronted with establishing new goals. It has always been a dream to play Massey Hall and it was better than I had hoped by miles! I actually think it was the best time I have ever had onstage and I must admit it's hard to keep going when for a moment you believe the best is behind you!

We finished the trio record during my time off in June and July. We are now proudly called Shaye — a namesake and living tribute to Tara's sister who was taken from this earth last May. We love the record and are becoming more of a family every day in preparation for the ride we are embarking on. The record comes out in October and we start a Newfoundland and Labrador theatre tour shortly thereafter...

I finished a new video for "Traffic" last week, again with Benji, who directed "Another California Song." The video is simple and sweet and enhances the song nicely. I have been having a difficult time catching up on my e-mails and phone calls because I have been so busy and I don't really see an end in sight.

I just returned from Jasper on the weekend — my Lord it was so beautiful. Driving in was like a scene from a movie with a fire raging to the left of us blocking out the moon and the stars; it felt so primal and that feeling didn't leave when we were told it was a controlled burn.

The Jasper Heritage Folk Festival was fantastic and it was again a treat to get to sing "Afterglow" with Tom. What an amazing gift to be able to sing that song in front of Tom's audience. I joke about how I don't make music with an eye for wanting commercial success, but after the first time I sang backup on "Life Is a Highway" I changed my mind. Completely unbelievable to see an audience from that perspective — totally freaking out! Tomorrow, Thunder Bay...

August 28, 2003

Thanks to all the people who came out for my first in-store appearance. It's hard to believe I have been doing this for eight years and have never done one before. Ah, the concrete floor on my bare feet, the fluorescent lights in my over-caffeinated eyes, and *books* — millions of them! The staff were a treat, so kind and talented (writers, actors, etc.). One even tried to "steal" me a gorgeous pic of Michael Ondaatje (my fave) from the café — it was a fruitless caper, but I did get a great cappuccino.

I met some genuinely lovely people today and I thank you for your kind words and commitment to music — I hope to see you at the Eaton Centre tomorrow!

Oh, and heads up for Shaye's first single "Happy Baby," which is being added to radio stations every day...

September 6, 2003

I snuck into the Toronto International Film Festival's "schmoozefest" last night by way of the red carpet; I guess no one thinks you are on a covert op when you're coming through the front door! I have been going to music parties for ten years and I used to love the excitement, the rush of meeting new people, but I'm like an alley cat now, there's no one left to meet. So it was fun to go last night and be mineral-free (unjaded, I mean).

On my way into the building, a really young, sweet, homeless man asked me what was happening inside and said he supposed that was where all the important people were. I looked at him and said absolutely not, it's the other way around. Of course, at that time, I didn't know *Neil Young* was going to be there. I worship Neil Young, I admire his creative vision, his ability to blur the lines between artistic mediums, and his devotion to his family. On my way to the bar (for friends of course) Neil and his wife Pegi passed in front of me and I felt the urge to yell "Keep on rockin' in the free world!" Thankfully I didn't, but hell it would have made a good story... I might need to rethink the ending.

I'm going to a meeting tonight with the girls and our new video director. Things are getting very exciting with the Shaye record. People are just starting to hear it now and they are liking it.

There were quite a few people there last night who have heard the single on the radio and loved it! We have our first gig (a private show) and a photo shoot this week and a video the next, and then I believe we are off to the races...

November 23, 2003

    I'm on a flight to Vancouver with the girls — so many pictures I haven't taken, things that have happened that I have already forgotten. I want to remember every minute, every moment, every particle, every strand, and every quirk of those I love... There is sadness, acceptance, and a state of feeling my dreams are just that — better on paper than reality.

    What a gaping hole Carlo Spinazzola created in Cape Breton when he left this earth....

Got myself a heavy heart
For the world today
Fixing up a solid place where my feet can sway
To the last dance of the night before the lights go down
I'm gonna take a dive in this fight
I can't go another round

Holding court behind your eyes
In constant conversation
Rumours of your demise
They don't rival your creations

You still inspire
Still making plans
Sleeping on the couch
Painting with your hands

Sometimes to quiet the devil
You're gonna drown a couple angels

December 3, 2003

I just might be the oddest person I know — a walking dichotomy. In the past year, I have done nothing but perform for people full on, but when it comes down to it, I am painfully shy and reluctant. I love to jump on artists' web sites, read their journals, and indulge in the tiny details of their day, but I am so hesitant to divulge my own. I realize it's been months since I have written, yet I have enjoyed the most fascinating months of my life with lots of wonderful things to share. I guess it's another quirk I get to lump in there with not liking sand between my toes, not liking raisins, and never taking pictures...

A good thing about being in a band: observing the traits of your partners and damn well stealing them. I guess that's why I bought a disposable camera last night at Shoppers and took inane pics of Tara and Kimmy driving to a Wal-Mart convention at 6:00 this morning. I mean, what else are you going to do except years later look back and go, wow, that was fun, glad I have a snap...

I can't remember the last time I heard a song once and had to have it, but today I saw a music video for The Darkness. This dude is an 80s version of Freddie Mercury — my jaw is still on the floor it rocked so much. Then I saw my friend Danny Michel smoke on *The Mike Bullard Show* — wonderful music thanks to brown camaros.

Our next Shaye single is a cover of Crash Vegas' immaculate "On and On." I remember when I first moved to T.O. almost ten years ago and my girlfriends came to visit me on McCaul St. We played that song over and over and over. It's fun to be able to play my favourite songs. Another good thing about this band is going back to the belief I had when I was seventeen; that I can do whatever the hell I want.

We had a fantastic tour on the East Coast — unbelievable houses and ridiculous responses. It's fun being in a band that gets standing ovations every night and very satisfying to share that with your best friends. Those of you who have seen the band know how stellar our musicians are: our wonderful musical director Kevin Fox (or Herbie the Love Bug as I like to call him), Pete Fusco (the most incredible dancer on the tour — Picco Piquant), Stuart Cameron (my coffee-making, East-Coast-by-way-of-Markham, fave neighbour), and Blakey Manning (this is a drummer not afraid to let me cut his hair while drinking Black Horse beer at the Hill O'Chips Hotel — not a wise decision probably, but a loving one). You've seen them dance; next tour, they'll get down to their Skivvies...

Kim and I got home to Nfld. and Tara to P.E.I. and then we all got to our home away from home — Cape Breton. We love the people there and we want to thank them for being so welcoming to us at such a hard time. Cape Breton lost a noble and mystical man in Carlo. A man so pure of heart that everyone who was fortunate enough to cross his path will mourn his loss now and then rejoice in his memory forever... Godspeed to his family, friends, and to Tina...

Maybe I have been reluctant to share because there has been such sadness in the last year and a half, losing so many young people so fast. We will miss Steve Hoffman because he was such an individual. Kim, Tara, and I loved Steve and we want to thank his family for allowing us the privilege of saying goodbye.

Now I am preparing to expand my journeys to Afghanistan. I leave Sunday, December 7th for Kabul with Rick Mercer, Tom Cochrane, Kevin Fox, and a killer CBC crew. I will spend my 28th birthday in Dubai, what a thought... I believe I will have little sleep before then, for as my departure draws near my dreams become increasingly frantic and erratic — nothing a little jet lag can't cure. Off to sing about Christmas to those who won't see their families for miles, won't kiss under the mistletoe, and won't have the luxury of a post-turkey nap. I just want to get home safely to meet my little nephew Devlin Hyde Doyle — what a name!

Much love and thanks to you for reading.

December 8, 2003

One day before my 28th birthday and I am flying business class from Frankfurt to Dubai. I'm putting on the complimentary socks and trying to find the TV. Two nights ago, I was so freaked out about this trip to Afghanistan, I stayed up until 6 a.m., ran home, packed (sort of), and got to the airport by 7:30. Needless to say, I was a wreck on the plane, caught a cold, and was a mess when my dear, sweet brother and sister — whom I haven't seen in two long years — met me at London's Heathrow Airport. I do believe, however, that I never would have made it on the plane otherwise...The mind can do terrible things — I think, therefore I am...at times a complete and utter basket case. Now I am en route and believe that once you commit to something, you just have to do it and enjoy it...

Later...

I'm flying over Bucharest and the moon is fluorescent white, the sky a hazy blue folding up into purple — simply the most magnificent thing I have ever seen. Its beauty decimates any fear I have ever had...

December 9, 2003

I am happily ensconced in my hotel room in the crazy city of Dubai. I have a mixture of jet lag, a head cold, and general queasiness due to an extreme lack of sleep and a solid meal...

Today was unbelievable; the gold market, the big bus tour, and a questionable visit to an Indian vegetarian restaurant (well worth the adventure). Spent the best birthday ever — no stress and no pressure. I have never been happier to be in a hotel room organizing things (which is very Kim Stockwood). I can't quite believe I am even thinking this, let alone saying it aloud, but I am happy to be out of my hotel massage room. Kevin Fox (the one and only) bought me a massage for my birthday. And me thinking that this is a country where women are mostly veiled, I thought that it would be an übermodest massage...*nooo* way — the woman massaged parts of me I thought were illegal to touch in Dubai — very, very strange.

Kev just came to my room with cards from my friends and family, an awesome package from Sheri and Wayne (the best in the world) with this beautiful journal, vitamin C, hand cream, sanitizer, a penlight, Fisherman's Friend, and, of course, chocolate. My dad sent a beautiful poem that made me cry. So vitamin C, echinacea, and, tomorrow, Afghanistan!

December 10, 2003

We're leaving Dubai for Afghanistan on Afghan Air. I must confess I am a little scared because the plane looks like it was used for stock film footage from the Second World War. That said, they could teach a thing or two to most North American airlines about service and free full meals — incredible. Now I sit next to a family of aid workers from Scotland — a couple in their thirties and their three boys, all under the age of six. This in a country so ravaged by war that aid workers are routinely assassinated as a message to world leaders. What kind of courage and conviction must you possess to not only place yourself in this situation but also to choose to raise a family there. It makes me excited for the opportunities I have been given in this world and to meet such selfless people. That said, don't use the washroom on Afghan Air...just take my word for it.

December 12, 2003

I'm sitting in junior mess at Camp Julien watching Afghani musicians play in front of the Christmas tree. This book is not big enough to write down all of the wonderful experiences I have had in the past five days. But I have to talk about the helicopter ride; it was *the* most amazing experience I have ever had in my entire life. Cutting and punching through the mountains at breakneck speed, the resounding khaki colour that permeates every stone and grain of sand, spotted with the occasional turquoise burka... So close to the earth, you could see the colour of the cow's eyes. As soon as I hit the ground, I felt so much taller.

Upon return, there was the small matter of mine and Moya's tent being demolished by the buzz of the chopper. That's what pictures are for. I'm trying not to mention, for my parents' sake, that I narrowly missed incineration. Good times at the mines, I like to say.

A view of the palace from Camp Julien.

December 13, 2003

We're leaving Kabul International Airport and everyone is sneezing, a by-product of too much disinfectant I suppose. There are few words that I could string together that would come close to describing the sandbag of emotions that is gripping my body: elation, pride, sadness, sorrow, hurt, sore eyes, and self-awareness. Knowing how much visits like these help morale is overwhelming. As they had upon our arrival, a fleet of soldiers escorted us to the airport in tanks, bearing arms and wearing flak jackets, helmets, and serious expressions. So I was completely overcome with emotion when we were presented with pictures of the troops and special coins reserved for outstanding deeds. It was slightly inappropriate to let the tears flow, but when I need to cry there is no holding back the sobs. I have a deep sadness for all of the soldiers that give up their lives to patrol unsafe and otherworldly streets. They never know if they will return home at night. They are bringing peace to people that have been rattled and riddled by war, poverty, and in a complete cultural lockdown of music, religion, dress — everything one uses to identify oneself.

The beauty of the once-exiled Afghani musicians; oh, the life behind their eyes. Funny how they stared in disbelief and a bit of awe at me, a western woman in high heels, a black dress that showed my legs and back, and wearing makeup (I'll never need another compliment in my life). To know how poverty-stricken they are and what a daily struggle it is to feed and shelter their families. Still, when CBC tried to pay them, they refused three times before they relented, even though CBC's union scale for one show is the equivalent to an Afghani's annual salary. Their dignity is exhibited not only in every facet of their behaviour but also in their dress. They arrived in thin, Americanized, blue jackets only to reveal pristine white shirts and pants accented by stunning, multicoloured embroidered vests, and all of them wearing their pride and honour on their actual sleeves.

The respect the crowd genuinely gave these musicians was the most heartwarming thing I have ever seen. I think everyone was a little nervous at how the Afghanis would be received when you weigh the psychological effects of war on a group of people. So the looks on the soldiers' faces with hands on their hearts, clapping and clapping for what seemed like hours was the most beautiful thing I have been witness to. The way the men held out their instruments to the crowd as if to say thank you for helping them to live freely and honestly in their own country makes me so proud to be Canadian. Peacekeeping has to be seen to be believed; the theory behind it is so unbelievably selfless. I hope I don't forget the faces and names of the people I have met here when I see them again, and God knows I'll need some help with that one...

I am changed forever and I thank my lucky stars...

A view of a bomb-riddled palace in Kabul, close to Camp Julien.

Mountains of Afghanistan; me freaking out.

A moment of peace and joy in flight (a short moment).

Post-flight jubilation.

Kevin Fox, Tom Cochrane, and me.

The wreckage of my tent; I'm so glad I got out when I did.

I survived, but my makeup didn't. Somewhere in Kabul someone's got a full makeup kit from MAC.

The Afghani musicians in full dress — so beautiful.

January 2, 2004

I have never felt such sorrow in all of my life —
 the whole thing
My heart is going to swell up and crack within my
 chest
My lungs are all at once out of air and bursting at
 the seams
I settle as I write this
I sobbed in bed tonight, big earth-shattering sobs
All inside the confines of my bed
Disappointment bigger than any ocean
Just one tear salts the whole sea

Everything changes when you have been given the extraordinary gift of being able to see the world in a different way, and you want to share it. It's devastating when you realize for most people it has to be seen to be believed.

March 9, 2004

So much has happened in these last few months that I have actually had a journal mental block — Afghanistan (simply the best experience of my life), meeting my new nephew at Christmas, the East Coast Music Awards, Canadian Music Week... I don't know where to start... For now, some words in memory of Cpl. Jamie Murphy from Newfoundland whom I had the honour of meeting at Camp Julien:

A man walks alone
his feet crunch the hard sand like snow
the only noise for miles
for the sharp slap of pre-dawn air
like a movie you saw about the war, but colder
so cold, you don't believe it even when you're
    there
in shorts and shoes you walk to the shower
guided only by memory and a northwest star
two months to go, then Christmas, now just
    nine more days
counting backwards on fingers and toes
it's going to be over soon
no chance you're not going home
those thoughts are long gone now
not like the first week
when you would cry into your pillow and think,
but I'm just a boy
To be a man making peace in wartime

To walk in those shoes
To ride in that jeep
To die not only for your country but for the
    whole world
To be a man making peace in wartime

In the mess hall with some fantastic Newfoundland and Labrador boys including Jamie Murphy (top row, second from right).

May 28, 2004

I just finished a great acoustic rehearsal in my living room with the Shaye band; the sun is shining and it's the weekend. What could be better than that I ask. We have a very busy summer lined up and for that I am excited. We're opening for Dido in Toronto June 8th and 9th, Jann Arden at the end of June, and Nelly Furtado in July. That's some serious female talent from around the globe. I just want to soak it in, close my eyes, and listen to three of my favourite artists sing "White Flag," "Unloved," and the glorious "Try." Good Lord, Nelly's vocal on that song is one of the best I have ever heard.

I just got back from Florida shooting a CBC Colin Mochrie special — what a kind and generous guy. We shot in the Universal/MGM lot on the New York City–street set, Kim playing a grand piano and our band members sneaking smokes in between takes while saving their instruments from the spray of night rain (okay, a hose to make the streets look radiant — oh, the movies).

I returned happy with some freckles and too many shoes (at a certain point one should seek treatment). My bandmates and manager pointed out that they have set a date for my intervention and it's in the fall, so even if I can't pay my rent, I can buy shoes safely until then! As you can tell by my lyrics, I often don't write when I am happy for I am too busy being happy to write, but things are good and that's quite nice to say out loud...

It is most exciting — *Davnet* is being released in Japan in July by JVC and I plan to visit there in September. I cannot wait to experience this beautiful culture first hand.

October 4, 2004

Fall is here, surrounding me like a big duvet. Squirrels have invaded the crawl space above my apartment and I am eating more than enough to give me that extra layer against the cold. Earl Grey tea and Nag Champa were created for days like this — to give the oncoming winter some romantic appeal. Easing in the change of season is the new Sarah Slean record, which has been squatting in my CD player since last Thursday — perfect music for the day. I only wonder how long I will be able to ride my new bike until the snow falls.

My $15 beat-up flea-market find is the source of my greatest joy. To appreciate such a basic thing for the first time in adulthood is like entering the wardrobe in Narnia. A whole new universe opens itself to you as it has been lying in wait for your age of discovery. Growing up in St. John's, bikes appeared to me only as devilish devices designed to unnaturally bulk up your quads for all the hills. As a child, I didn't touch the things at all.

When I first moved to Toronto, I went and did the grown-up thing and bought an expensive, shiny, forest-green bicycle that sat challenging me daily and it scared the hell out of me, naturally. One day, after years of neglect, I decided to set the bike free and left it leaning up against my building unlocked. For three months it sat there taunting me. This in a neighbourhood where bikes were stolen from underneath the bums of babies and sleeping grandmothers; perhaps it was thought to be a sting. I know for certain no one will steal my new bike, but for other reasons entirely.

    I had a great summer — great music, great people, and sunshine. At a certain point as a woman you have to ignore advice about never showing your face to the sun. Personally, I would rather see Madonna's face a little wrinkled than the waxed-pallor look she's sporting these days; a happy face needs a little sun. Speaking of happy faces, we had a great time with Nelly Furtado on tour. What a wonderful person and performer with a great band and a great crew. I watched every single show side stage and loved every minute of it — spectacular.

    Shaye is off to Halifax this weekend to play with Symphony Nova Scotia and hope to see you there. In the meantime, I am trying to learn some Japanese before my trip to Tokyo in a couple of weeks. Gordie Sampson and I are heading there to promote our latest solo records and hopefully write a couple of songs on the plane... Actually, I am going for the food...

Shaye at a performance with Symphony Nova Scotia.

October 19, 2004

It's 9:30 in the morning and I have been up all night packing, planning, and getting more and more excited about going to Japan! I am on a flight from T.O. to Detroit and was so happy to get an emergency aisle seat next to two beautiful Japanese people, but they had to be moved (so rudely because they didn't speak English). Now I am stuck with a loud page flipper and an elbow bumper, the wife incessantly talking to her husband and he never responding and I mean not ever, not once. Did I do something bad to deserve this?

I went through a full strip search at check-in today — more thorough than in Afghanistan, where as a woman you were brought into a separate room and groped. And since it was the last point for currency, I also emptied my pockets and gave her all of my money. Needless to say, I felt a little dirty walking out of that room I tell you... Anyway, it'll be good to hook up with Gordie and our manager Sheri Jones in Detroit, sit next to each other on the plane, and pass out the whole way to Tokyo...

The flight was long, but not half as cumbersome as I was fretting it would be. I had slight panic when I realized that not only were we not sitting together but I was wedged in between two strangers. Thank God one of the gentlemen switched, and I nuzzled next to Sheri for fourteen hours. I slept most of the flight, thankful for the awesome neck pillow and eye mask from our Juno gift bags — I will always travel with them from now on.

When we arrived, Takashi Udono from JVC met us and took us on a peaceful train ride from Narita to Tokyo only to realize we had landed in a typhoon — unbelievable! We met an associate of Takashi's at our train stop and the five of us lugged all of our gear up from the station through the madding crowd to our hotel elevator. If they had only known how much luggage we would have (not to mention Gordie's 60-pound guitar case), Takashi would have brought 100 associates to help. Poor Sheri, I thought she would wipe out about ten people at a time with her suitcase — it was so funny.

Buying treasures of hope and luck for my family at a temple in Tokyo.

Performing at the Canadian Embassy in Tokyo with Gordie Sampson.

Me with Takashi Udono from JVC eating out again!

Sheri, Gordie, me, and Takashi sightseeing in Tokyo before the jetlag kicked in.

Me, Sheri, and Gordie starting to feel the jetlag in Tokyo.

Mica (my wonderful translator), me, TV interviewers, and JVC staff.

Me with a Japanese journalist after a two-hour interview — one of the best in my life.

December 9, 2004

I am an hour and a half into my 29th birthday and, surprisingly, I am smiling and peaceful. It's not that I find growing older depressing; on the contrary, I find women get better with age, like good wine or that chocolate in the back of the cupboard you've forgotten about. So when I take the time to really look in the mirror, I find I actually like the things about myself we as women spend so much time trying to cover up. I like the lines on my face, the spots from the sun on my arms, the weary glint behind my eyes and I love my freckles... These physical marks serve as a reminder of the best moments of my life. Of sunning myself on the top of a caravan in Dubai exactly one year ago; of braving my face to the storming heavens while walking through the gardens of a beautiful shrine in Tokyo with wonderful friends new and old, only to find a break in the typhoon-scarred sky; and of drinking one too many mojitos exactly where Ernest Hemingway did in Havana. Maybe in a couple of years I'll let my hair go grey, but not just yet. I've got Spanish to learn, pottery to perfect, and a couple of albums to write... Oh, and I need to buy a new bike, the damn thing got stolen. I loved that bike, but to be honest I am quite flattered someone thought it was worth stealing... Musta been the Kathleen Edwards sticker.

Kim, Tara, and me celebrating Tara's birthday as a family.

December 10, 2004

Well, I turned off my lights for you Rick Mercer... Rick has my vote — I will act because I trust him. He hasn't strayed from the path, he hasn't blatantly abused the powers afforded him by celebrity, and he hasn't taken advantage of our television-smushed minds. Hopefully Canada will listen and will begin to conserve our precious energy resources and live enlightened in the dark.

I was only happy when the snow fell two mornings ago because I was no longer in a state of mourning. My little bike with the Kathleen Edwards sticker was actually stolen. The bike I thought to be unlovable except by me and surely too rusty to make a mad dash down Queen Street has been pried away from its lock and spirited away... The first snow has fallen and I'm already thinking about Spring (Yes, Spring with a capital S). My next bike will have no mention of Kathleen — that's probably the reason they took it in the first place. Damn sticker...

Me and the stolen bike with the Kathleen Edwards sticker — irreplaceable.

December 15, 2004

I'm at home in the middle room of my mom's house in St. John's — white sheets, white noise. When I was a child, I avoided the dark, damp recesses of my basement. The unfinished floor with jutting rocks anchoring the washer and dryer, the furnace a perfect hiding place for fugitives and monsters, but tonight I snuck downstairs to bravely fetch the summer fan. The fan — why would I need a fan at this time of year in Newfoundland of all places? The white noise. I fear I cannot live without it.

At 1 a.m. I woke up in the eerie silence of my childhood home, no furnace buzzing or humming — nothing! Now I write in my cooling bedroom, which will be freezing in no time at all. My thoughts drift to impossible circumstances and places where there would be no fan to speak of; how would I ever sleep? The arctic, the desert, the Days Inn?

A splitting headache is accompanying me to bed tonight; it feels as if something is about to burst in there. Waterlogged (or alcohol-preserved) veins and muscles from the middle of my back to the core of my head — ready to blow. Tomorrow, I will exercise like a banshee. It was not a good sign when the first thing I ate upon

arrival was chips and salsa — excellent chips though, I must say.
    Am I tired yet?

December 16, 2004

I enjoy the little things in life so much more than the big things, like a good cappuccino and the smell of a wood stove. Too much work and energy goes into the big things, it leaves precious little time for enjoyment. I know when I am old and grey (whoa, am I ever gaining fast in the grey department) I will stand on a stool somewhere and wave my arms frantically as I hold my whiskey glass (with two pieces of ice and a drop of water, thank you) and share with the world my favourite things in life. At the top of my list will be the hot-water bottle my mother put into my bed at night without fail whenever I stayed with her. I cannot express how much this hot-water bottle means to me — for so many reasons.

I finished Michael Winter's new novel *The Big Why* last night and really loved it. Newfoundland has produced some fantastic writers in recent years; Michael Crummy, Lisa Moore, Wayne Johnston, and the list goes on. In fact, two years ago on New Year's Eve, Ron Hynes was playing the Ship Inn and, one by one, I met them in the bathroom, by the bar, and on the dance floor. One by one I gushed and said how much I had enjoyed their books. (Really — they were among my top five books internationally for a two-year period.)

So, hopped up on Christmas cheer, I marvelled at my luck to press the flesh of my favourite authors all in one night. Then I slowly turned to see they were all sitting together at the Ship's famous, dark, corner table. Then the paranoia I am prone to suffer set in like a chainsaw — they think I'm full of crap. They've swapped their encounters and subsequent compliments from me, and they believe me to be a lying, brown-nosing fool who's probably never even read their books — "Sure, she probably can't even read, she doesn't really write those songs herself, and, to top it off, she doesn't look a thing like her picture." That night, like every other New Year's Eve before, slid sharply downhill. I am just thankful I didn't end up in St. John's Harbour...

That said, I think Michael Winter's new book is brilliant.

December 18, 2004

Today I made no ritual observations. Nothing struck me as peculiar enough to write down. A kind of glove, a sort of weariness...

I have seen Karma do its work
It is exact, so precise
It is the unprettiest thing I have ever seen
So tired, so sad
Lest I not receive what I want Karma to enact
Be good girl, be good

A girl's best attack: echinacea, exercise, and the odd Advil...

December 24, 2004

A.M.

    I went to a great party at my friend Claire's last night — the food was spectacular. Unbelievable that she could even pull it off, let alone with grace. My Lord — the ham, the shrimp, there's no wonder I feel so big today; you are what you eat and at this rate it's not pretty. Not to mention the homemade cheesecakes and cookies; she should really think about catering. That would be a good combination: a nautical engineer/caterer...

    My girlfriends from high school are an eclectic bunch, I tell you: an air traffic controller, a doctor, a dance teacher/studio owner, a teacher/counsellor, an engineer/seamstress, a lawyer, and me, a musician. All you'd need is a couple good restaurants and you've got yourself a town. Looking forward to having everyone safe and sound in Newfoundland for Christmas tonight. I am off to wrap some presents...

P.M.
Christmas Eve, counting down the hours, a prayer
    upon my knees
Sitting, waiting so far away
Alone, watching the numbers
Change the signs that scream delay
A storm upon the dreams of being home

F***ing JETSGO

Arwa, Claire, Gillian, Stephanie, and me — friends since high school.

December 25, 2004

Not a single gift wrapped. The Newfoundland-bound flight abandoned in Toronto and my sister alone in New Zealand, across the world. I awoke this morning puffy-eyed to hear my nephew crying in the hall. Really, my eyes are almost swollen shut, I haven't had a good cry like that in years and I don't believe I am done. I can always be counted on to count my blessings, but I am dead last depressed I tell you. I think my heart is going to crack — crack wide open...

How can a corporation do this — cancel Christmas — so thoughtless, so many heartaches, where I am the least affected? The shots of people on television — entire families stranded trying to get home, including a single mother travelling alone with two babies, left with no word of an explanation, not even an apology — nothing at all. Do they know what Christmas means to Newfoundlanders of all people? They left hundreds of people alone in the Toronto airport on Christmas Day — they obviously don't have a clue who they are dealing with.

December 28, 2004

People in my life have left this earth in the most extreme and tragic ways imaginable — too little air, the carelessness of half a second, another's hand, and their own. Through this I have learned to live fully, as if any day that too could be my fate. Life is better now with the knowledge that there can be peace and acceptance in death and life.

How can you find the good in this Tragedy?
The babies, the bodies; oh, the bare bodies
Not only ringed hands and feet,
But piles of cadavers with bare bottoms sticking
    right to the top

Who was that man?
Is there anyone left alive to look for him?
Had he held respect where now he lies naked
With no dignity for miles?

I am swollen from Christmas overeating while we watched people on television dying in front of our eyes.... Why aren't we there yet? It is all about swift action, cut the tape, stop discussing, stop strategizing, stop vacationing, stop scanning the surface, stop following, and lead. Follow your gut, not protocol...just get there.

January 2, 2005

I woke up choking today from a dream where I was choking. The weather is doing the strangest things. It is eight or nine degrees Celsius today, raining and resembling nothing of January. I miss my family; it's so strange to be back here in Toronto after the tsunami and trying to figure out what to do.

January 4, 2005

I just found out I get to go back to Japan for the World Expo with Shaye and I am so excited I could scream. Somehow I am going to have to be excited enough for two people (three actually), because Kim is going to be close to seven months pregnant then and just under the cusp of flying restrictions, so it is going to be pretty challenging for her. I can't even begin to imagine how daunting it would be to tour so far away from home when you are that pregnant — what women do is pretty incredible... I know there is no way she would even considering going if it wasn't for Tara and me, so it's safe to say I feel a little responsibility... Thank God for the lore of the women who would endure childbirth only to return to the fields to work or else we'd be all in the running for sainthood in our own minds... Those are the stories that keep us sane.

January 7, 2005

    I pity the ones that choose to walk the earth with a split heart;
    Those people who live a life they know is false and sad. It will ultimately be recognized as their tragic flaw.

How many times have we all done it?
Been too tired, deflated, and duplicitous to not
    make the hard decisions in life.
To lead a false life is theft — not only to oneself,
    but everyone involved.
You're not doing anyone any favours...

January 8, 2005

It's been a very emotional week back in Toronto. Traditionally, I find the first week of January inspires despair, lethargy, a nervous breakdown or two, and, if I am lucky, some very depressing songs. A small consolation is that everyone I know is usually in the same boat — someone to hold on to when you are drowning. They too, of course, are drowning, so we will either tread water together or draw straws in fending off the sharks.

My appointed role for this week's play was Heathcliff — my apartment, Wuthering Heights circa 1986 (the fixtures anyway). There were many pots of tea and listless walks to nowhere. Where do you go when it is so cold you can bottle your breath but there is no snow to catch your footsteps?

Well, you fly in the face of all accepted teachings of how to ring in the new year! Yes, you make New Year's resolutions but you do as I did and resolve to eat more than you did at Christmas, drink copious amounts of red wine (the cheapest brand you can stomach as the Christmas bills are rolling in), and exercise once — yes, once and only once; it's going to carry you the whole week. Whatever you do, do not unpack. Just pick random items from your suitcase (like the new sweater you coveted so) and throw it in a ball on the floor with the rest of your delicates. Don't even think about doing laundry or sending the Christmas gifts you didn't have time to send before you left. And do not, I repeat, do not download the proper software for your digital camera so you can see all of the gorgeous pictures of your two-year-old nephew who lives in England and you won't see again until next Christmas.... You see, this last part is crucial. If you disobey this rule as I did just a second ago, it will be your downfall for properly ringing in the New Year. Trust me, if you actually see these pictures you might die of a broken heart, and it's not even close to Valentine's Day.

My nephew Devlin, loving my new iPod.

January 10, 2005

There is a mouse in my apartment. I have seen the top of its head poking out from behind the fridge, scurrying quickly down the hall, and seemingly straight into my feet. Not a very smart or tidy houseguest let me tell you. Perhaps intuitively it knows about the ridiculous array of high-end cheeses I have leftover in my fridge from New Year's Eve.

I cannot bring myself to do it in even though it is having no problem doing that very same thing to me. I feel like a heroin addict coming clean; as jumpy as a cat, thinking everything is moving and out to get me — talk about paranoid. I saw the end of my hair tonight while washing my face (of course my hair being black and, well, hair) and thinking it was the mouse, I jumped back about five feet and got soap in my eyes and then I screamed for real.

Anyway, it's just not a good situation. You would think I would be used to living with rodents. When my sister, Ceara, was going through her all-black phase in high school, she brought home a pet rat named Zoe. It would have been alright if we didn't share a room and she wasn't committed to keeping the rat's existence unknown to my mother. Needless to say, things didn't go my way there for a few years.

With all of the best intentions in the world,

our dad sweetly bought us a state-of-the-art ghetto blaster, which had automatic tape reversal. This was a tremendous novelty until year two of listening to my sister's tape of the Depeche Mode song " Somebody" over and over again on a blank tape that would change sides automatically throughout the night.

During this period, Zoe lived in a cage in our closet (when she wasn't at school with my sister), constantly taunting our cat Higgins who knew she smelled a rat. Higgins would scratch and claw the bedroom door all day long to no avail and I think that's what really made her go crazy. I was thankful, however, that she stopped clawing at me for a while (a childhood phobia that lingers to this day). Every morning, from age seven to fourteen, Higgins would lay in wait while I quivered down the hall, and every morning like clockwork she would jump out and attack my arms and legs. Very traumatic, I tell you.

Ceara bought Zoe as a tiny little thing at the pet store and I don't think she was anticipating her to grow a foot and a half long. That's no life for a rat in a cage, so Zoe had to find a new home. I actually blocked all of that out until I just saw the top of my mouse's head. I can't handle paper cuts, let alone knowingly sharing a room with a rat. Needless to say, my sister is a very powerful person...

January 15, 2005

I'm just waking up from CBC's Tsunami Relief Benefit Concert and I don't even know where to begin. So much has happened in such a concentrated period of time that not only am I having a hard time truly digesting it, my shoulders have seized up around my ears. The tendons in my neck are like guitar strings, every ounce of tension I have felt is being held right at the base of my spine. I wait like an unfinished plaster bust for any passerby to chisel my shoulders down to their rightly stature. I swear a chisel would feel good on my actual muscles today. I would probably smile; I am what you would call a smiler — I smile through the pain. In fact, if I am smiling, chances are I am in physical pain and if I am frowning chances are there is nothing wrong with me at all.

I think my physical pain is a manifestation of needing to write, needing an outlet, the drop-off after the peak, the pinnacle, the precipice. I need to play my guitar, I need to get out of the house and get a Starbucks coffee — oh, the addiction weighs bean after bean.

January 19, 2005

Well, life is so strange. So strange indeed — designed to disappoint.

I can't seem to do anything but obsess about my personal life and it's getting so boring, so painfully boring, yet my writing is flowing. Maybe that has been the catalyst, the icebreaker to writing all of the time. God knows I need to do more of it — writing, not obsessing, that is.

"I should be writing!"

January 25, 2005

Oh the great wrinkle in the design of a musician's life. Flying, not flying, waiting, rushing, fearful, and then grateful.

First things first, being from Newfoundland, I have an insider's understanding of inclement weather. If you are smart, you cushion in a day on either end of a trip for storms, mechanical failure, and basic communication breakdowns between customer and customer agent.

It is Tuesday at 2 p.m. and I have been trying to get to Toronto for two days, where cockily I did not build a cushion into my schedule — rats. So after my flight was delayed seven hours and then cancelled, I rebooked for the direct flight this morning at 7 a.m. I will always choose an inconvenient time over stopovers, since the taking off and touching down are the most taxing parts of flying.

So I went to bed at 2 a.m. and then tossed and turned, battered around the work I should have done in T.O. yesterday, checked the time repeatedly and then after a cool forty-five minutes' sleep, I woke at 5:15 a.m. to get to the airport. I checked in, the flight was delayed half and hour, got in line for Tim Horton's, and the flight was delayed another hour, so my father and I decided to bolt and I went to grab a nap at home.

Stupid, stupid, stupid — never leave the airport, they are the ones in the know, not the reservation agents. I called at 7:30 a.m. and they said my flight was cancelled. What they didn't mention was that it was combined with a flight at 10 a.m., as I later learned, that was not cancelled. So I called to rebook and I have lost another working day. It's now 5 p.m. and I am taxiing down the St. John's runway writing with a shaky hand and two little slits for eyes as I have a had a grand total of two hours' sleep in 48 hours. It always makes me nervous when the pilot comes on and says we are going to taxi slowly because of the excessive ice — not very reassuring, I tell you.

Airlines all have their own little quirks — the flight attendant just told me that in order to have my sweater over me I would have to put my arms through my sleeves backwards. I mean, you couldn't make this up as a comedy sketch if you wanted to, it would be too absurd.

How stunning the sun is when you have given it up for dead.

Just like always, as soon as we took off from Newfoundland I wanted to go back like I had missed something.

January 29, 2005

The earth has shifted on its axis this past month. The physical changes have subconsciously changed everyone who gets out of bed; a month of walking this altered earth has in turn altered us. People have taken an active role in humanity. Anybody who has cried knows they have cried for another; those that have given know they have given; they who have hugged their children a little harder, hug them harder still. We that tread the earth know it is a privilege and we will be grateful for as long as we can hold on to it.

There seems to be so much to do in a day, it creeps up and then it is gone...

I have been out of school for twelve years and to this day I am firmly rooted in the September-to-June, Monday-to-Friday mentality. I rage against it; still today is Saturday and in a sense I feel free of any obligation to work even though my work doesn't know the bounds of Monday-to-Friday living. Not that I could work anyway, I have new housemates living in the apartment above me. Where before I heard not a peep, now I hear constant and heavy movement. The curse of apartment dwelling, above, below, and to both sides. The walls tremor with the reverberations — what in the hell is going on up there? I think the guy is actually creating beats, all I can hear is the same bass line over and over again.

The mouse is now in my bedroom; it is so tiresome. The idea of being able to call your landlord about such things is fantastic, but when the landlord doesn't come or do a thing for weeks and months on end and the ceiling has caved in, and the freezer is broken (six whole months), it doesn't seem too peachy. The only thing I can do is unpack my suitcase from a week ago and pretend I am in a dance club — a very bad dance club.

February 1, 2005

Well, the countdown is on to write and record this Shaye record before Kim's baby comes in July. What a delicate balance mothers must find, so we are trying to get as much done now as possible. We went to Ron Sexsmith's today and sat in silence (as silent as we birds can actually be) as he played us some song ideas on his piano — what a transcendent experience... In times like these, I count my blessings for the life experiences alone...

February 3, 2005

I am lying in bed in my favourite hotel, the Westin Ottawa (where the heavenly bed is truly heavenly), waiting for room service and watching *The Ashlee Simpson Show*. My two guilty pleasures, this and *Newlyweds*. They hold some sort of car-crash, side-of-the-road fascination for me, as do most cable shows. The best thing I have ever done in my life was to get rid of my cable; unfortunately, it rears its ugly head in hotel rooms.

I just got off a plane from T.O. where I sang the national anthem for the Empire Club's presentation of Newfoundland's feisty premier Danny Williams. Danny gave a fantastic speech that received him a standing ovation, the likes rarely seen, from a group of people (with the exception of the Newfoundlanders in the audience) who went into the situation without truly understanding the tragic history of the rape and pillaging of Newfoundland's resources. It was incredible to see the looks on people's faces as the premier spoke with such passion, determination, and knowledge and swayed them one by one — fantastic.

These are the too-few-and-far-between hours that highlight a touring musician's life; you enjoy the hour of downtime like it's really good and non-addictive crack. I never write this stuff down because I am too damn busy enjoying it.

February 13, 2005

Sometimes things get so busy and information accumulates like compost — eggshells, banana peels, coffee grinds piled on top of each other, then one day you realize it has turned into soil. My emotional digestive period is quite long, it takes a lot of processing to turn it into something palatable. Then one little thing will hit me and I will cry for everything at once.

I just turned on the TV and saw the Janis Joplin tribute with Joss Stone and an incredibly ballsy Melissa Etheridge. My heart stopped when I saw this little, shorn creature walk onstage with an electric guitar. Now this is a woman who has done so much for gay rights, adoption, and girls with guitars, but what she did last night for all women was incredible. With so many entertainers possessed with regards to their appearance, the most beautiful woman ever walked bravely and bald into the spotlight...

February 15, 2005

I've been waiting for hours for my bags at Pearson International Airport and a person just walked by wearing a T-shirt with the slogan "A list of reasons to procrastinate." Of course there was no list but I: a) picked up my notebook to write as I had been putting it off all day when b) my bags arrived. Typical bus-stop-smoke law of the universe reaction.

There is some odd sense of security flying Air Canada; actually, I know exactly what it is. It's the possibility that one could, by some miraculous teardrop of fate, be bumped up to first class and today I was — well worth waiting the extra two hours to get my bags, I say. Ah, the legroom and cookies. I guess you need the extra room when you are eating so many cookies!

February 17, 2005

I'm so excited to be invited on CBC's *50 Tracks* by my friend Jian Gomeshi... Hmmm, what in the world to pick? There are so many great songs from the 80s (the decade I am a panellist on) and I have been wracking my brains trying to narrow it down to ten let alone two. Well, it kind of helped that someone else picked a Leonard Cohen song and I couldn't pick "Hallelujah," so it left "Lovers in a Dangerous Time" by Bruce Cockburn and "Sonny's Dream" by Ron Hynes, and these are my reasons:

"Lovers in a Dangerous Time":

This song should be playing in delivery wards all across this crazy world. How can you bring a child into this world without hope? How can you welcome it without the acknowledgement of the place we live in and a willingness to do something about it...

Largely believed to be about the emerging AIDS crisis in the 80s, this song feels as if it was written about souls colliding in Rwanda, Somalia, Lebanon, or today in Iraq. However, the seed of this song is an image of kids in a schoolyard who are bold enough to go and hold hands in the face of having no future. Bruce Cockburn is our wandering Canadian soldier — keeping peace, raising awareness, all the while writing devastatingly honest postcards of the dire straits of our world. But there is always a pinprick of light encouraging us to mobilize ourselves off of the couch. Never preachy, never pushy, just inspiring.

Why "Lovers" and not "Rocket Launcher"? Because everything he writes shares a political back story. "Lovers" has such an infectious melody and lyric: Bono heard the brilliant line "Gotta kick at the darkness till it bleeds daylight" only once on the radio and he borrowed it for U2's *Rattle and Hum* album. The first time Canadians saw The Barenaked Ladies they were riding in the back of a pickup truck, freezing their butts off in the middle of winter singing a song about love in wartime. What is more relevant to the entire world than that?

Our Newfoundland national anthem "Sonny's Dream":

Ron Hynes is a living legend; he is also a friend that I have a healthy dose of bewilderment of. For what beast beats inside this body to repeatedly create four-minute masterpieces? Is it the soul of James Joyce washed upon the shores of Newfoundland or an earless Van Gogh destined to be deified after his time has passed?

For Ron's crowning jewel "Sonny's Dream" is so well known around the world, people assume it is a traditional Irish folk song. It has been covered by dozens of international artists including Mary Black, Christy Moore, and in the great Canadian spirit of oral tradition it was passed along and recorded by Emmylou Harris (who was surprised to hear the author was alive and well and living in Paris, only one of the outlandish claims found when you Google " Sonny's Dream"). Not only is it Newfoundland's unofficial anthem, it is an anthem for all those that left the lands of our forefathers to seek a new and better life across the seas to Canada. It is a song of longing, love, and the sadness of being responsible for a generation. And when voting, remember the wrath of Newfoundlanders when they have been wronged...

(Revised note: both songs made it into Canada's top 50 tracks!)

February 25, 2005

It's my brother's birthday and at 12:30, it's too late to call England. Damn time change, and his wife Robyn's birthday is just two days before. I just cannot seem to get birthdays right. Just because I avoid my own means I slip responsibility for others. (No excuse, I know.)

Kimmy (and her precious and precocious bump), Tara, and I got together today at Kim's place and decided on the twelve songs to demo for the next record. There is a feeling of otherworldliness with the group, as if Shaye herself is guiding us to create something great. She is there in harmony, always keeping us together.

This past weekend was the best East Coast Music Awards in eight or nine years and, of course, it was in Cape Breton! I saw so much of the Sampsons (Frank, Amy, and Gordie), but sadly not enough of Flo, who went on to hijack the piano at the Quality Inn. Gordie swept the night as he deserved to. I've never been so happy to lose so many awards. Again, just as my intuition told me that after virtually no trying I'd come up with a name for the band (Shaye), I prepared the girls for not winning a single award (not one out of five). That said, I'm betting Kim's having a girl. My intuition I trust, but it has been ruined, ruined I tell you, by what Jewel said in her song "Intuition." I saw some great music by the Trews and I was blown away by Katherine MacLellan (Gene's daughter) at the P.E.I. room at the Cambridge Suites.

The award show itself was nice and intimate, so much so that Rita MacNeil was sitting right in front of us for her tribute and when I looked down and saw her sitting beautifully in her blue dress as I sang the line "you were never oh so blue," I burst into tears. I must admit I was just carrying on my behaviour from the rehearsals, for every time Matt Minglewood sang "Working Man" and the Men of the Deeps came onstage I was on the floor crying. At least I was able to stand up straight and finish the song for the live telecast.

Rita's story of overcoming adversity and triumphing against all of the odds gets me every time. I remember walking into Rita's Tea Room about ten years ago, seeing the picture journey of her as a young girl to her on world stages and I cried then too. So seeing Matt and the Men of the Deeps sing "Working Man" was the highlight of the show for me, as was turning to Kim and saying "Is that Belinda Stronach over there?" Very strange, you just never know who you'll run into in Cape Breton.

Me with Kim and Tara before performing a tribute to Rita MacNeil at the ECMAs.

February 27, 2005

Oscars, so exciting! It's been six days since I got back from Cape Breton and only today did I unpack my suitcase. Ridiculous I am, clutter only begets chaos — personal chaos.

If I lived in a bartering world, I would trade my abilities as a housecleaner (to a moderately clean person, of course) in exchange for them coming once a week to sort, launder, dry clean, fold, and hang my clothes. It is really astonishing how I can obliterate a hotel room in ten minutes! Then I go over to Kim's room and she will have everything laid out in order. I recognize this is a choice, a test I fail 80% of the time; slovenliness usually wins.

I had a lot of factors riding against me this week though. The biggest and most unexpected obstacle was *The Da Vinci Code*, a book I have refused to read based solely on the fact everyone and their dog is reading it. The same reason I rent big blockbusters at the DVD stage. Hype almost never pays off, so I wait until it has subsided and passed me by. Between separate testimonials from Tara and Gordie, they convinced me to read this book.

Well, it's been a long time since I've read a book so gripping, so intriguing with all the elements of a soap opera villain's wedding. So much so, I have had to sneak into bedrooms and bathrooms to read it. The other night I had a good friend visiting from out of town and instead of getting ready for dinner, as I was pretending to do, I snuck into my room, cuddled under the covers, and devoured as many pages as I possibly could until people came looking for me. I finished it yesterday and thankfully my life could resume — what a mess...

We wrote a lot last week; the pressure is on now after debuting our first new song at the Songwriter's Circle at ECMA. "Travelling Light (Now You're a Star)" is a song we wrote with Gordie about Shaye looking down at us as we all look upon her, now a star.

Shaye is, of course, Tara's sister who was taken from this earth almost three years ago. Shaye was a great actor, singer, and writer who on her path to lighting a flame so blindingly bright she became the floodlight for us all.

The day of her service was the most beautiful I have ever seen: twenty-eight degrees Celsius, the coast of P.E.I., red clay caking our feet and covering our legs. There has never been quite a celebration of life as that day, and Shaye was holding the cards. We actually sang for the first time in public that day, Ben Harper's "Shall Not Walk Alone" and for the whole rest of the day everyone sang like it could save us.

Something I will never ever forget was seeing her casket. It was unfinished and unvarnished and Tara got brightly coloured markers and everyone who passed through the wake line was able to write a parting message to Shaye. Without knowing, Kim and Tara wrote exactly the same thing on opposite ends of the basket (as Tara likes to call it). Something to the effect of "I always thought you were going to be a star" and now she is a star. Every time one of our songs comes on the radio or our name is said aloud or used in print she is shining on, our goddess of light.

March 1, 2005

Snow has covered Toronto like a wet woollen sock — no army yet, but you can tell people have a defeatist attitude towards it. Then I think of the mountains of snow in St. John's the last time I left; now that'd get a body down.

We are off to work again with the original muffin today, Ron Sexsmith. It's funny how the songs are really shaping up in this last week; I can actually see a record. We are going to start demos next week with Stuart and Kevin, and we're very excited to start. Japan is in six weeks. If I started today, I could complete the six-week Japanese course book. I really should do it; I just have my doubts I'll be able to find the time. Where in the hell does all this time go? Last time I looked, twenty-three seemed old — crazy.

March 2, 2005

Moral dilemma: we must add on an "oh baby" or add a verse with the lines "smack my ho around" to the song we finished with Sexsmith yesterday. We must take a perfect gem of a song and make it a hit. Anything at all to earn enough money to get a facial like the one I just got, each and every single month. So you are moving along in your life with the delusions that you are of the earth and not at all materialistic because you don't feel the need to dry or style your hair for months on end (until you see yourself on television and then the curling iron comes out). Then you go and splurge and go to the nicest salon in Toronto, Canada probably, and instantly you have the curse of the fabulous woman.

Not only do I need to have a facial, I need every inch of my body polished, buffed, and restored — NOW — no matter what the cost.

This is bad — very, very bad indeed. How do you justify such an extravagance when there are people begging for money to feed their kids on the street corner, please let me know.

Kim came to pick me up this morning and got stuck on the ice in front of my house. Me pushing, she five months prego, and this able-bodied man just walked by. Nothing — he didn't even look up, he just kept on walking. It's not like he didn't notice the sputtering car and me all of five-foot-five trying to push it. That's what sucks about Toronto; people won't go out of their way to help people the way they will at home on the East Coast. It's like they have their blinders on at all times, afraid to let down their guard. I mean, Tara jumped out of the car yesterday to help someone push, for God's sake, and to her credit, she got the guy off of the ice.

March 3, 2005

The sun is splitting the rocks out there!

For the first time in my life, I have just heard a song that I have been a part of writing sung by somebody else on the radio. What a wicked feeling to help birth a song and let it go out into the world without my guidance and without my worry. Anything seems possible today...

March 13, 2005

It's been ten days since I've written and now journal writing has taken a similar role to that of exercising, songwriting, and singing. If I don't do it, I get incredibly anxious — good for my publisher, bad for my mental health. Just another thing to keep me neurotic. Ah, the anxiety is leaving my body already.

I had a great Canadian Music Week experience, seeing everyone at once. It's no wonder industry folks have conference burnout. It was everything I could do to not go out Saturday night: I wanted to so badly, but Sunday morning at 7:00 we had to be at the airport to go to Vancouver to play a private gig. We don't do a lot of corporate shows but we are perfect for them. First off, this was a grocer's convention with nothing but food samples everywhere — anything and everything you could dream of. It was like dying and going to food heaven. Absolutely fantastic. Not to mention meeting our namesake baby, the daughter of our fantastic EMI rep Gary and his wife Lisa. Such an honour for us, as they named their baby Shaye.

We have been doing pre-production (trying out arrangements) for our record with Kevin and Stuart all week and my brain is mush. Now that I think of it though, I believe my brain is mush because I have been watching the *Godfather* movies all weekend. Those movies are like a colonic for the mind, it flushes it all out.

March 14, 2005

Marianne Faithfull was appallingly good tonight. It was a last-minute thing to go to the Mod Club. I was in no mood to go out at all; I really wanted to stay in and organize my apartment. It's so odd, last week I went out every night and now all I want to do is stay in. I feel so clear-headed and ready to work. I can't wait to get into the studio tomorrow with the girls; I am so excited to get it on paper, as it were.

A million things weighing on my mind, mostly taxes — I am going to start right now! Bye bye.

March 15, 2005

I did start my taxes. It's unbelievable really, that never happens. I must be procrastinating, though I am just not sure what from. But this doing taxes thing is really a life Draino, getting things out where they should be...

We started demoing the new Shaye record today. Bloody fantastic. The three of us (four when you count Kim's baby) singing together in a tiny room. Not even Tara's car getting towed for a cost of 180 bucks could ruin our spirits.

I had a great pottery class — I am in my second term and believe I am actually regressing. During the first term, I was a star, hot off the sprinter's block like a pro only to slowly run out of speed by this term. Out of breath with no grasp at all. There are just so many fully encompassing creative things going on in my life right now that I haven't been able to strategize what to do next. That's the type of person and potter I am, I spend the first half of class plotting my actions, the second half executing them, except for this term, I haven't known what to do next.

But tonight in my second-last class (too bad, so late) I got my groove back and, like in first term, was the last one to leave class. I have just been so busy playing, writing, and recording that I've had to leave class early and arrive late. In another life, or maybe later on in this one, I would love to study, truly study, pottery as I would Spanish.

First, I must stop watching scary movies, they have turned me into a complete neurotic. I've always had a bit of a reclusive and somewhat suspecting nature, but yesterday morning it reached new heights altogether. The night before, I watched *The Professional* with Jean Reno and a very young Natalie Portman, a recurring theme is the innocent knocking on doors and subsequent slaughter of men, women, and children. So when I was lying in my bed trying to coax myself out of the covers, the dreaded doorbell rang and rang and, again, rang and rang. I was too petrified to even look out the window to see who it was, I just lay there hurdling between *The Professional* and *The Godfather* in my mind — frightening combination.

I ran late to an appointment an hour later only to find the FedEx, "sorry we missed you" slip on the front doorknob. When Gavin de Becker said to believe your fear, I'm not sure he meant me. I think I need a personal consultation.

March 16, 2005

I just went to set my alarm for the morning and a new Gordie song came on the MIX 99.9 FM and it sounded great. There is a pride that comes when you see your friends doing so well. We ran into Kathleen Edwards and Colin Cripps (he produced her new record and they got married last summer) at Terroni's (my absolute all-time favourite T.O. restaurant). I had so much pride watching her kick ass on *Letterman* last week, and I barely know her. I feel truly blessed that I derive as much pleasure (or more) from the successes of those I love and admire than I do my own.

I have seen people eaten alive by jealousy, competition, and insecurity. It will all be as it will be and I count myself fortunate to know that in my bones, fingers, and toes... Everything changes at karaoke, however, when people can be viciously competitive — frighteningly so. I am actually glad that I am a substandard karaoke singer. This comes with a level of competition I have never seen and won't see again until I go back to George Street, St. John's and step into someone's home turf — the reigning karaoke champion that doesn't relish new blood; they sniff it out and hunt it down. Besides, it can be just too much fun — the type of fun that doesn't let you get out of bed for days afterwards....

Another mouse — this is getting ridiculous now.

March 18, 2005

I am in Old Montreal for the weekend redeeming a very generous Juno-nominee gift certificate from the Hotel Gault. You could say I am stretching out the honour of being a Juno nominee for almost a full year. I believe it is better to be nominated for one and lose than it is to win five in one year because at least you are able to truly enjoy the benefits.

After driving for six and a half hours, we arrived happily to find a gorgeous duvet, huge feather pillows, a heated bathroom floor, and a charming staff that lead us to a great restaurant on St. Bernard next to St. Laurent. My friend Jaelyn and I shoved enough food into us to feed eight grown men, not to mention the wine — a seriously needed girls' weekend. Unfortunately, our cab driver, who was very sweet, had no idea where our hotel was and a very comic and expressive cab ride ensued. Now safe and happy under the covers, full of water, and watching the ultimate *What Not To Wear* $50,000 dream trip to Paris — I could not be happier.

March 19, 2005

It's Saturday night and I am lying in bed drinking a Cosmo in a fancy robe in a hotel room that is not my own. Now don't get the wrong idea, everything is on the up and up. Life has a funny way of bringing you what you need when you are able to articulate it. Walking back to the Old Port from a long day of beating the streets of Montreal, I twice said aloud the only thing that could improve my weekend was a bath, but sadly there was no bathtub, just a shower.

So back at the hotel I tried to open my door with my key — and nothing. Then the manager came with the master key; it could not, would not, and still hasn't opened the door (the bathless room). They immediately shuffled us to a room next door, a room with a *huge* bath. So here I lay post-bath, drink in hand with all of our things locked in the room next door — absolutely everything — and I couldn't care less, I am so happy and tired.

Just goes to show you, when you are on the road you aren't really seeing a place. I have spent about six months of my life in Montreal, but it seems like I am seeing it for the first time since ten years ago when I soaked it up like wasabi. What a fantastic city, phenomenal people. Imagine eye contact, people actually looking at each other in the eye — wondrous. I thought of

Leonard Cohen and Mordecai Richler and the wealth of life, art, and history. Of course, Cohen and Montreal wrote *Beautiful Losers*. The dark underbelly of Montreal is its brightest side.

March 22, 2005

Exhausted. Dirt tired. So tired it hurts to lift my hand to write.

First off, last night I changed my bedroom furniture around by myself. And I am talking heavy furniture, but I must admit it is one of my favourite things to do. It's like getting a new apartment, but today everything hurts.

I went to the studio early today to record some guitar parts for the song called "Travelling Light" or "Now You're a Star." Deciding on titles and where commas should be (Tara's favourite thing in the world) gives us much delight as a band, never dull I tell you. Then I got to record Stuart playing some guitar; there is so much power when you are the one who gets to push the actual physical buttons. I admit, I love it so.

Then the girls came in and we recorded vocals, then I was off to my saving grace Moksha Yoga that was created by our good friend Ted Grand. I literally have not been cold or had a cold since I introduced his practice of heated but open yoga into my life. This is coming from someone who used to wear a parka in the summertime; my internal temperature has gone through the roof. Then I ran late to my last pottery class. A busy day where everything I did was an extreme privilege and for that I am so grateful...and hungry.

March 23, 2005

Yesterday, spring paid us a visit! Then it went to get a glass of water and never came back — no note, no call, not even a rumour of its whereabouts; a full-blown, cold-case file.

In its absence today was a slow-moving train with barely enough coal to take it out of the station. We wrote with K-Fox, also known as Kevin Fox. I'm so glad to be going to work with people I love. I can't even imagine the sort of person I'd be as an unhappy employee...

The coals appeared in the writing of a beautiful song called " Falling for It," one of the best I've been a part of ever. It's funny how the song actually came about. We were all at Kim's house doing pre-production and as I was going to the washroom, Foxy started playing this gorgeous thing on the guitar. I started singing in the washroom and when I came back out I said, "Can you play what you were playing before I went in the washroom?" There and then we began "Falling for It" — that's going to be a fun story to tell if it's a hit...

I saw a bunch of actor friends tonight playing funk music at Clinton's, their conviction was outstanding. If only I could play like that sometimes, or do I? Well, if it was funk, maybe. No, I don't think I do, actually — actors, absolutely incredible.

March 30, 2005

I feel like a prisoner in my own home, trapped by mice.

I am going crazy, every noise, every little, teeny, tiny sound gives me a fright, the complete heebie jeebies.

Today, the traps came out. This was something I was very reluctant to do, as I really didn't feel it was my place in the universe to decide that these animals are an annoyance and I should get rid of them. I have changed my tune, I tell you. Let me first say that before this drastic measure, every crack between the floors and the baseboards and every little hole was filled with steel wool in an effort to keep them out of the apartment. So when that didn't work, it was last resort time — hence the traps.

For example, is that a mouse, is a mouse digging a hole through my wall? Not fun questions to be asking yourself. Seriously, though, I wonder if that's my dryer... It's too bad, I love this apartment, but it's over, the mice have spoken.

We wrote with Hawksley Workman today and had a genius time. What a fantastic fit, the four of us; a little bit of magic I think.

I'll take peace within now, please.

March 31, 2005

    Anxiety-riddled carcass, through to the core. Everything seems to be unravelling somehow, or is it? Am I letting it?

Confusion, a grey blanket,
Living only in memory
Fading colours
The tape gets worn down
Every day, hoping to see

April 7, 2005

So often I have to force myself to write about positive things because when you're having the time of your life, you are simply too busy being too happy to write it down. Then when that lull comes it hits like a free-falling elevator, sinking fast into your boots.

The light-headed joy descending and heavy, making towards the ground, drawing on all of your organs, the blood drained from your face, your neck, and right out of your fingers and toes.

Suddenly, you see you've reached the bottom and you didn't die after all — not one broken bone, not even a single scratch. So in the morning, when the daylight is fresh and clean, you push the button that may not take you to the penthouse, but it does get you to the lobby.

One would lose sight of joy if it wasn't cradled in sorrow. Yet sorrow can be used as a hit of indulgence, especially when it affects others. That all said, I had a great weekend in Winnipeg for the Junos.

I cried an unbelievable amount this weekend. It started with k.d. lang singing Cohen's "Hallelujah" and Neil Young's "Helpless." Helpless, helpless — oh, my heart is still racing thinking about it. It was quite simply the best performance I have ever seen. From the balls of her feet she sang — with every tissue, every perfect fibre. Never have I seen song and singer married in such perfect fashion. So that started my weeping — open broad-faced sobbing (the stewardess on my return flight brought it up because she had been sitting right beside me during the show — great).

I thought the crying had stopped until I saw Leslie Feist at the EMI after-party. I haven't seen Leslie in about two years and not since *Let It Die* came out (which is, in my opinion, one of the best records ever made). I just went up to say hello, but no, I started to bawl while in her arms. I am now sure I felt a million times worse than she did when her guitar completely hit the fritz while she was standing in the middle of a jam-packed arena by herself, not realizing the show was live. She, of course, handled her situation with amazing ease and grace and pulled it all together and came out on top. I, on the other hand, was a complete mess. It was almost like I was watching a movie; I was completely invested in this character and all I could do was sit and watch her walk straight into the lion's den. A lot like the scene in *Boogie Nights* where Mark Wahlberg storms into the drug dealer's house — I actually had to leave the theatre I was shaking so much. I then proceeded to tell her how much I loved the record and I just could not stop crying. Poor girl, having to spend any part of her Juno-winning night consoling me…

April 10, 2005

There is a beautiful release that comes with saying the truth out loud, so cathartic and clean in these walls of water. I feel light, bare, and exposed to the world, vulnerable to attack, but so, so open to what the world has to offer.

April 12, 2005

I am not sure exactly how long the small and large intestine is when combined, but the whole of my insides have contracted in the core of my body.

Music is barrelling through my head and down the back of my spine at ninety klicks an hour.

Truth is springing from my mouth at a breakneck pace.

My past in my face, like a chalkboard regenerating itself when wiped clean. The same prophecy in different languages with different translators.

The coffee eating at my nervous system until there is nothing left but a brittle osteo-riddled skeleton.

College Street construction. The sun making freckles and warming babies and I am right back where I started. I see the sun and know my power comes from its core, but it's too hot to touch and always will be. Will my skin harden to where I can reach in and grab it, take what I know is mine? I am sure, and when I am sure, the soothsayer in me is stoic in that knowledge. The details are sketchy, but the truth remains.

I wish I had it in me to drop my laundry off somewhere, but I can never quite bring myself to do it. The laundry piles higher and higher until I actually have an extra hour, but I always use that hour for something else. A quick aside showing that tackling the simple things in life could actually relieve some chaos.

Back to the chaos and curse of knowing what you want and not being able to have it. It won't magically go away; it eats and gnaws like a hungry dog, digging a hole you can scarcely get out of. I say scarce, but it feels like never, though never is not allowed here in my life. I thank Lucinda today for making the music that crushes a soul. Listening to "Car Wheels on a Gravel Road" is like taking two Advil, it dulls the pain just enough to make life manageable.

How do you paint a picture of life when you have refused the offer of canvas and paints?

April 16, 2005

Sometimes life catches you in its cradle. You are mothered, babied, fed, listened to, and cleaned up after. I have the best friends in the entire world. Up there in the grand scheme of things, friends are my greatest accomplishment. In that sense, I am wildly successful.

Change is scary, but so, so exciting when you know you have done everything in your power to make things work. The universe, however, sometimes has other plans for those of us that wander these grounds. There is a reason for everything that happens in this life and there is peace in that for sure.

Today I did yoga on the top of a boathouse in twenty-degree weather with not a single cloud in the sky on Lake Muskoka. Truly one of the best experiences I've ever had. A gorgeous walk in the woods, great food, and great company with Tara, Ted, and Sophia.

April 21, 2005

I just took off from O'Hare International Airport in Chicago en route to Nagoya to play at World Expo with the girls. Kim and I rubbed her big belly on takeoff and told the kid to stay in there for at least a couple of weeks. Even if things did happen prematurely on this flight, I rest easy because I know Tara was a midwife and doula in another life. Everything would be all right, but that said, the baby should stay put at least until July 1st.

I am so excited to be going back to Japan. I love the people there so much, and my last trip there left such an impression upon me. So now a crash course with my Japanese language books. I really wanted to have a better grasp on the language for this trip, but you can't do everything and we have been so busy...

I should be fast, fast asleep. Five hours in and why can't I sleep? Usually I am a sleeping pro in these situations. I've got my eye mask, my neck rest, and I'm well fed. I should be out like a light. I am actually hot and that never happens to me on a plane. I have to say the service has been outstanding and everyone polite, unlike my last long-haul flight from Japan.

The last thing in the world I want to do right now is to write and prod into my inner world, partly because it seems like such a huge relief to be going so far away from it.

It is so much easier to live life skating on the ice instead of spending all of your time excavating the memories that are drowned and frozen beneath it. In fact, don't even glance down at the faces glaring at you through crystal clear ice. The problem is, without looking down, you can't see where the ice grows thin, where one false move will put you under too.

I have my grandmother's blue, wool-knit socks on. I have so many pairs and each one I cherish with all of my heart. Now there's an object you can actually love — a pair of handmade socks. Wow, I just looked out the window and I saw Alaska, God how lucky we all are. Wouldn't it be amazing to get plunked down in Anchorage just for lunch? Geographically, it is so odd how Alaska is a part of the States and not Canada.

Jumping around in exhausted thoughts, I'd give my eyetooth for a little, teensy pair of scissors. There is nothing like natural light this close to the sun for spying split ends — anything to keep my mind off of my swollen feet. I am suffering from a salty lunch. That and the altitude is making my skin feel like it's going to crack. I should know better from my momma, the woman who teaches her love of the high road like no other and also to stay away from salty foods. This because when she was pregnant with me, she almost died of toxaemia (not the Britney song). Her doctor immediately ordered her off salt and said she would most certainly die if she ingested a single grain of salt. So began her intense obsession with mustard and ground and cracked pepper... I got the love of salt.

We just crossed the international dateline, right under Siberia in the Bering Sea. Oh, the world seems so accessible when you are soaring above it. My travelling companions are very funny people high on Valium, Robaxacet, pregnancy, *The Da Vinci Code*, and sleep deprivation. Eight hours in and no one has slept. I was even laughing out loud at *Friends* — very sad.

There's one hour left and I am officially ready to be off of this plane. Kim and I are as swollen as the Flintstones and I'm not even pregnant.

April 23, 2005

6 A.M.

The sun is splitting the rocks and we are six in a tiny (large by Japanese standards) apartment all waking up one by one as our bodies try to assimilate to the daylight... I'm a little depressed really; as beautiful as Nagoya is, it can't really compete with Tokyo, which is so exciting and vibrant — oh, I loved it so.

Kim is eating crackers in bed — so hilarious. The things you never learn about someone when you always have your own room. Things didn't help when we went to an American-style diner as soon as we arrived. Put it this way, the most nutritious thing on the menu was deep-fried Spam. Who in the hell wants to go to an American diner as soon as they arrive in Japan? Not a group with two picky eaters, two vegetarians, a vegan, and a pregnant woman. But I decided to go with the flow, even though when I am on the road I can spot a bad restaurant coming from a mile away. But sometimes that makes me a little too bossy and fussy (a very bad road combination), so I was trying to relax and change my tune a little. The only edible thing on the menu was tortilla chips and salsa and I was served Doritos and ketchup. My only recourse was to have three nutritious Asahi — at least I know that's good.

Today I am awake with plans of exploring; right now, it's all about food and avoiding a nap. I miss the bright lights, so I must get on a subway and find them.

6 P.M.

We're rehearsing for our first show tomorrow. Everyone is jet-lagged and, of course, mildly affected, and I mean that in a politically correct way. (It's a good thing I have it all on videotape.) I am the official unofficial Shaye videographer, which means when we edit the tape all together, people will be like "Oh, yeah, there used to be this third girl in the band, but I've no idea who she is." I'll live with that in exchange for all of the fantastic tape I have of the girls doing and saying things I might be able to sell on eBay.

I went back to sleep this morning until 11:30 a.m., then set off in search of some touchstones, mainly Starbucks and shoes!!! Ah, shoes...

10:30 P.M.

We struck out in the food department for a second night in a row. Raw eggs don't appeal to anyone in the group — not a single one of us.

April 24, 2005

Life is not good when food is bad. It's 5:30 in the morning, Kim's baby is kicking like a mad woman, and we just heard a mighty crash. Tara had just snuck into our room laughing about trying to be ever so quiet but instead bringing the house down with crashing dishes. So I take it back, life can be good with bad food.

Bad food can also give you nightmares...

My dear I cried a mile for you
To know I awoke with fear
Nightmare of your face
It didn't look at all like you
My memory had been erased
Still the folklore of my heart reads
You were the one that got away

April 26, 2005

Now the jet lag is gone and life is settling in with some normalcy here in Japan. World Expo is pretty extraordinary and continues to be a wonder that can never fully be explored. Allergies have kicked us all pretty hard here with the changing of the season and the highest amount of pollen in the air in twenty-five years. That's a photo op we must jump on while we are here — the three of us with our pollen masks on, allergic to each other ostensibly. I only developed allergies three years ago April, and, of course, for the first year, I, in my old hypochondriac headspace, convinced myself I was dying of a brain tumour. That feeling of allergies seizing up your ears, neck, eyes, and throat and filling up your lungs is doubled here in Nagoya. Kyoto, on the other hand, leaves you gliding, just floating on the surface — a most extraordinary place. If you have any doubts at all about the environment and your part in preserving it, you must visit here and you will find a way to recycle every last thing you touch.

We took the two-and-a-half-hour trip to Kyoto by van with nine people. Kimmy and Sheri stayed in Nagoya (too pregnant for the hills, but never for shopping) and set out first for a Buddhist temple. It was quite a steep walk up from the parking lot; a fifteen-minute trail littered with beautiful pottery stores, kimono shops, fish stands, and coffee shops. Coffee for the ritual of it, of course. Silly me, I asked if I could find a take-away cappuccino and received alien-like stares. I don't know if it's taboo to drink on the walk to the temple or if they don't do take-away cups.

Miraculously, symptoms of my coffee withdrawal disappeared when I rounded the corner and I saw the temple entrance in front of me — I didn't need another thing, just that. After the initial impression of awe wore off, I remembered I had been dying to use the bathroom for about three hours. Once again, I was in Japan desperately needing to go and there was no bathroom in sight. Two things Japan needs more of: bathrooms and garbages. (Revised note — the last thing they need is more garbages, for it is expected that everyone takes responsibility for their own mess and will recycle almost everything — brilliant, I say.)

The most stunning thing I have seen on the whole trip was on the drive to Kyoto. Interspersed amongst the fields of rice paddies and gardens were the smallest of mountains. Built into the mountains were graveyards, peeking out from the rocks about three graves in and ten graves long, high above the earth and safe from rising water. Each time I saw one, I would reach for Tara's arm and cry. I would love to have a painting of that. Maybe I'll have to do my own.

A mountaintop temple in Kyoto.

Kevin and me in Kyoto. "A long way to go for some ice cream."

April 27, 2005

We had a day off yesterday and it was Sheri's last day here, so the four of us girls went to Japan's biggest orchid garden, a perfect respite in the middle of the city. We went upstairs and had high lunch. It was so peaceful; we sat for hours just soaking it all in. Times like that make me realize what an unbelievable reality show we could have. The four of us armed with the bare minimum of Japanese language tools, trying to order food and drinks without our lovely Japanese-speaking Akiko — genius comedy, I tell you. It's a wonder they didn't kick us out with all of the arm-waving expressionism that went on. Our poor waitress — if tipping were accepted in Japan, she would have got one big-ass tip.

After a day of shopping, Tara and I finally found the antique market we had been searching for. Twice a month on the outskirts of Osu Market and on the front walk of a reconstituted temple (Nagoya was flattened and rebuilt after World War II), a tiny field of treasures lies in wait. Where to start was a question that could not be pondered because by the time we got there everyone was packing up for the day. That, however, left us in a bit of a bargaining position. Language was absolutely no barrier here with cellphones spelling out the bartered prices. It made me want to go back and return everything else I bought that day, especially a pair of shoes that are borderline hideous. Looking at them now, I am pretty sure they are just wrong, wrong, wrong. But hell, they fit, and that's enough here in the land of little, tiny feet.

I found a beautiful, red, antique box that is presently lying on my bedside table. It is the most gorgeous thing I have ever seen along with a heavy, wooden, carved wall hanging. How I am going to get it back I don't know, and I don't care really. The crowning glory is in the form of two antique serving bowls that I hemmed and hawed over for twenty minutes because of a little chip and I have already used them for dinner tonight.

Speaking of dinner, Kim and I were craving a home-cooked meal and we set out for the supermarket, which was an adventure in itself — I loved the individually prepared celery stalk and the meticulous wrapping of minute quantities of fruits and vegetables. Having only one little pot and one little pan we still managed to cook up a feast, and we had nowhere to put it — except in my two new beautiful bowls!

Kim, Sheri, Tara, and me. A final lunch at the orchid garden before Sheri leaves for home.

April 29, 2005

We're back from our show — a hot, hot, hot day with so much pollen, Kim's eyes almost swelled shut. I'm back at the apartment lying in bed listening to my iPod (the mother of all inventions). There's a candle burning by my bed with incense from the Buddhist temple. Such a wonderful feeling; fatigue can be so rewarding.

Sometimes I think half the people must be at our show just to stare at Kim's belly. We walked around Expo today and everyone, I mean everyone, could not help but blatantly stare at this blond chick with tight clothes that looks just about ready to pop.

Karaoke with the staff at the Canadian Pavilion tonight...

April 30, 2005

Heaven falling
Like a blanket of snow
Covering the truth
For just a moment
Until the hellfire melts
There's not a dream of heaven left
Only certainty

May 01, 2005

I can honestly say I am feeling extremely stressed about compiling these journals for a book. I can't breathe; the anxiety is just about killing me. It appears to be an almost insurmountable task to compartmentalize my life. Plagued by questions of: Could this actually be interesting to anybody? Am I boring? Am I one-dimensional? Why am I putting myself in this situation? At last look I wasn't a masochist. In fact, self-preservation has always been a top priority for me. Now when I should be in Japan enjoying the experience, I have procrastinated to the point of staying up late at night trying to play catch up, all the while worrying about trying to represent myself within a hundred fifty pages. The only time I could forget about it was the other night at karaoke, which was fabulous. Lots of great people from the pavilion came out, including the Commissioner General — a fine singer, he.

Today it poured, but we did the show anyway — just three more left. We all felt like we wanted to go home today; just a sense of unease between the weather and the cramped nature of our apartment. So in the midst of the rainstorm, in typical me-fashion, I put on my sneakers, grabbed my iPod, and went out exploring into the Japanese night. I returned an hour and a half later soaked down to the bone, but refreshed and content. I do love this country so much. Wednesday, we are scheduled to have lunch with the Imperial Princess of Japan, which was unexpected and exciting. Kim, or, as she is affectionately known around these parts, Butterball, just did an hour of research on the princess, so we will be prepared. Tomorrow, Takashi from JVC is coming and I can't wait; he is such a great host.

Takashi and me. Finally, I found my beloved ebi tempura.

Me with Kim, Tara, and the little one in the belly at a radio interview in Nagoya.

June 21, 2005

I'm sitting in a writers' camp for the second season of *Instant Star* trying to piece together the last two months of my life. I'm happy to say Kim's baby is still in her belly and we have been anticipating the baby's arrival any minute now for the last two weeks. Needless to say, every time the phone rings I get a little jumpy!

The rest of our time in Japan was wonderful. People say that life changes at the World Expo and I think they are right; the planets and stars all align to create something perfect. There was a sadness in leaving Japan just as there was for me in the fall. It is such a gentle and peaceful culture. It's almost as though you have to go through an angst filter at the airport before you are processed through customs.

Our lunch with the princess was no exception. What a stunningly beautiful lady on all levels; she is so well spoken and has quite a sense of humour. She truly delighted in seeing Kim eat everything in sight with the fervour only a pregnant woman can have. (Okay, well, she hasn't seen me eat.) Tara was seated next to the Toyotas (yes, *that* Toyota). She got along so well with Mrs. Toyota — I believe they are planning on adopting her.

Things were full steam ahead after I got back jet lagged — writing camps, a beautiful visit from my father, a trip to New York City with my mother, and moving all in three weeks, not to mention finishing the Shaye demos (which sound great, by the way).

I have never walked so much in my life as I did in New York that weekend. It was a bit like seeing the city for the first time as I haven't been there since 9/11. The highlight of our trip was visiting the chapel adjacent to the World Trade Center site where people kept vigil for months and the workers and volunteers went to rest and get nourished.

I was not expecting how gut wrenching it would be as I am aware that desensitization generally occurs when you see horrific images on television over and over again. I also believe that this plays a big part as to why adolescents who have been raised on action movies, TV, and video games are committing violent crimes — life becomes fantasy, not reality. So it was incredibly overwhelming to be struck with such emotion when seeing the site of the towers from ten feet away. The chapel was even more intense since selected signs of thanks to the volunteers still hang inside, and, even more heartbreakingly, so do the "missing" signs with loving descriptions and pictures of happy-looking people. It was quite a long, slow, and silent walk back up to our hotel.

Thankfully, my mother was here to help me as I packed my apartment and waited for movers that were three hours late while the new tenants were waiting with all of their furniture on the front lawn. I can't even talk about it now; my heart rate is going through the roof just thinking about it.

The weekend I moved in, I got to go home to Newfoundland to play a benefit for AIDWYC, which is the Association in Defence of the Wrongfully Convicted. Never before have individuals and their remarkably unjust circumstances affected me so deeply. I know this is something I will want to be a part of my entire life.

The Newfoundland cases cut close to home with three stories on the table of men falsely convicted of murder. These men have to live not only with the memories of the excessive amounts of time of unjust imprisonment but also with how these convictions continue to muddy their names and reputations, not to mention how it affects the lives of their families.

It was mind-blowing to sit behind David Milgaard as his lawyer spoke at length about his case and the web of lies and deceit that was created in order to keep an innocent David in the horror of jail for twenty-three years, then to meet him and see him for who he is today: a beautiful survivor. Also, to meet Steven Truscott who, after decades and decades of hiding, is now opening himself and his family up to reliving the travesty he experienced when he, at fourteen years old, was sentenced to death. He has never been exonerated from this crime — a crime many know, and many knew then, he did not commit.

How can we live in this country and profess to live in a free and just society when we let this occur simply because it hasn't happened to us? I guarantee you that if the people who are able to rectify these decisions were thrown in jail for just one night, they would sing a different tune.

It's the first day of summer and I am ready for it, so ready.